GRACE BYERS

I Am Enough

PICTURES BY KETURAH A. BOBO

BALZER + BRAY
An Imprint of HarperCollinsPublishers

Balzer + Bray is an imprint of HarperCollins Publishers.

I Am Enough
Text copyright © 2018 by Grace Byers
Illustrations copyright © 2018 by Art by Keturah Ariel LLC
All rights reserved. Manufactured in Italy.
No part of this book may be used or reproduced in any
manner whatsoever without written permission except in
the case of brief quotations embodied in critical articles and
reviews. For information address HarperCollins Children's
Books, a division of HarperCollins Publishers, 195 Broadway,
New York, NY 10007.
www.harpercollinschildrens.com

Library of Congress Control Number: 2017938681
ISBN 978-0-06-266712-0

The artist used acrylic paint on board, scanned into
Adobe Photoshop with digital chalk backgrounds, to
create the illustrations for this book.
Typography by Jenna Stempel
21 22 RTLO 29 28
❖
First Edition

For eight-year-old Grace . . .
for God, Mama Cheryl, Faith, Alyssa, and Trai, my greatest loves;
and for You, the beautiful soul reading:
may you never forget how enough
your enough
truly is.
—G.B.

To my niece, Zahara, who always sees herself in the
characters I create. To Patricia, Thelma, and Cora for
being anchors and matriarchs and loving me unconditionally.
—K.B.

Like the sun, I'm here to shine.

Like the voice, I'm here to sing.

Like the bird, I'm here to fly
and soar high over everything.

Like the trees, I'm here to grow.
Like the mountains, here to stand.

Like time, I'm here to be,
and be everything I can.

Like the champ, I'm here to fight.

Like the heart, I'm here to love.

Like a ladder, here to climb,

and like the air, to rise above.

Like the wind, I'm here to push.

Like a rope, I'm here to pull.

Like the rain, I'm here to pour
and drip and fall until I'm full.

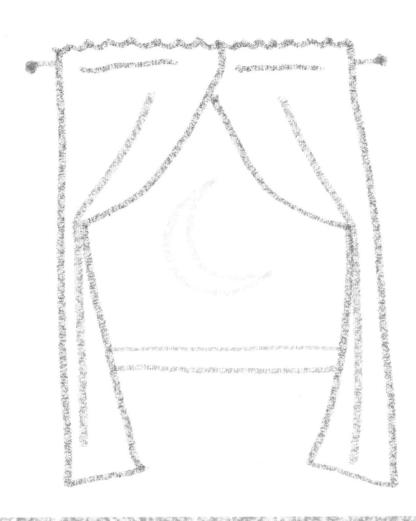

Like the moon, I'm here to dream.

Like the student, here to learn.

Like the water, here to swell.

Like the fire, here to burn.

Like the winner, I'm here to win,
and if I don't, get up again.

I know that I may sometimes cry,
but even then, I'm here to try.

I'm not meant to be like you;
you're not meant to be like me.
Sometimes we will get along,
and sometimes we will disagree.

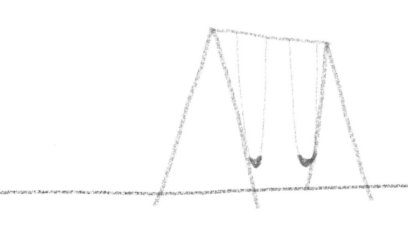

I know that we don't look the same:
our skin, our eyes, our hair, our frame.

But that does not dictate our worth;
we both have places here on earth.

And in the end, we are right here
to live a life of love, not fear . . .

to help each other when it's tough,
to say together:

I am enough.